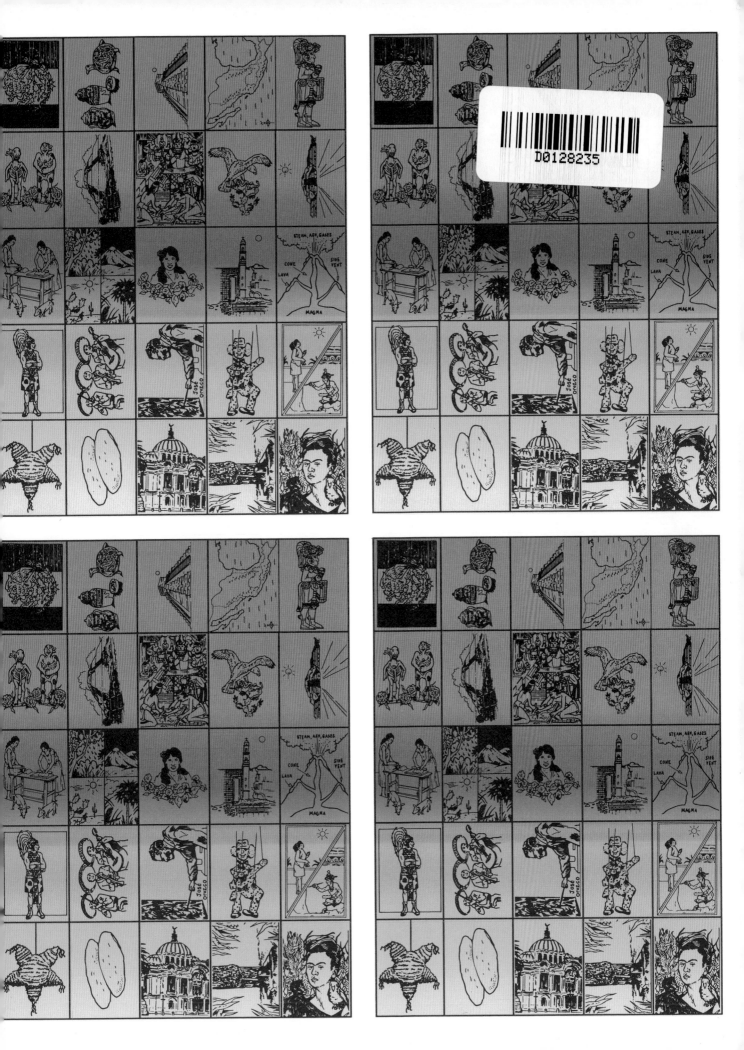

MEXICO

By
Jane Pofahl

Cover Illustration by
Mark Anthony

Inside Illustrations by
Marc F. Johnson

Publishers
Instructional Fair • TS Denison
Grand Rapids, Michigan 49544

Acknowledgement

Many thanks to Joel Revzen for providing me with the opportunity to sing in Mexico City with the Minnesota Chorale in the Palacio de Bellas Artes and at Teotihuacán.

Credits
Author: Jane Pofahl
Cover Artist: Mark Anthony
Inside Illustrations: Marc F. Johnson
Project Director/Editor: Danielle de Gregory
Art Production: Darcy Bell-Myers
Typesetting: Deborah McNiff

About the Author

Jane Pofahl has taught kindergarten through the eighth grade in Minnesota schools. She has worked with students outside the classroom as school yearbook and newspaper editor, play director, speech coach, and private tutor. Her biography has appeared three times in *Who's Who in American Education*.

Jane Pofahl lives in Apple Valley, Minnesota, with her husband, Don, and Buddy, the Wonder Dog.

Introduction

History is the living record of the human race—exciting as it is varied. *The Time Traveler Series* will aid you as you teach the colorful history and culture of countries around the world to your students. Explore such topics as geography, city and rural living, art and music, historic events, holidays, famous cities, and meet the historic personalities who helped shape the cultures of countries today.

After each topic is presented, activity pages are provided for your students to implement suggested vocabulary, conduct further research, and provide creative answers/solutions to historical situations. Fun reproducible pages are also included to review the historical and cultural facts studied on the preceding pages.

Each book contains the following:

- topic information pages
- research/activity pages (including maps, charts, research topics, and creative thinking activities)
- reproducible activity pages
- cultural stickers

The Time Traveler Series was created to spark the sense of intrigue in your students and lay a foundation for enjoyable history instruction and learning. Have fun!

Table of Contents

The History of Mexico

Mexico's human history began when nomads from Asia crossed the Bering Strait and traveled south through North and Central America before 8000 B.C. Native Mexicans lived in small tribes or communities and developed farming and trading methods.

The first known settled society in Mexico was by the Olmecs, who lived along the Gulf Coast from 1200 to 400 B.C. They were followed by the Mayans, who ruled the area from 300 B.C. to A.D. 900.

The Classic Period of the Maya existed from A.D. 250 to 900. Teotihuacán, a great religious and commercial center, was also at its height during this period.

Toltecs controlled the Valley of México from 900 to 1200. The Aztec Empire grew and flourished from 1325 to 1521, when Hernán Cortés and his Spanish conquistadores conquered the Aztec Empire for Spain. The superior weapons of the Spanish and the terrible diseases brought by the Europeans helped keep the native Mexicans under Spanish control for almost three hundred years.

On September 15, 1810, Father Miguel Hidalgo made his famous speech for independence, which rallied native Mexicans to rebel against Spain. Fighting continued until 1821, when Mexico won and gained its independence from Spain. In 1824, Mexico became a republic with a president, a two-house congress, and governors running the states.

By the mid-1800s, Mexican leaders had trouble with the northern territory called Texas. General Santa Anna tried to keep Texas a part of Mexico. Santa Anna led the Mexican army in battles at the Alamo and San Jacinto. Texans declared independence from Mexico and became part of the United States. In 1846, the United States declared war on Mexico; the United States won the war in 1847.

Santa Anna was forced out of power in 1855 by Benito Juárez. The War of the Reform lasted for three years, leaving the government almost bankrupt. Napoleon III of France invaded Mexico in 1864 and set up Maximilian as its emperor. Juárez and his forces captured and shot Maximilian in 1867. Juárez became president of Mexico again from 1867 until his death in 1872.

Porfirio Díaz succeeded Juárez, but many people hated Díaz's dictatorship, prompting the Revolution of 1910 which lasted four years. The revolutionaries won. The Constitution of 1917 guaranteed free public education, a 48-hour work week, a minimum wage, and the right of workers to strike for better pay.

In 1934, Lázaro Cárdenas was elected President. He took land away from private landowners and gave it to farmers. However, the Mexican people suffered from low wages while the population grew, so Mexico had to borrow money from foreign countries to pay its debts.

Money problems continue to trouble Mexico today. There is an enormous difference between the small wealthy class and the large, but poor, working class in Mexico. As well as money problems, Mexico City was hit with devastating earthquakes in 1985 which strained Mexico's money reserves even more. When the North American Free Trade Agreement was signed in 1993, Mexican workers rebelled because they felt that it would benefit the United States while hurting the Mexican economy further. The challenge Mexican leaders face today is to improve the quality of life for the Mexican people without forgetting the values and traditions of the past.

Geography

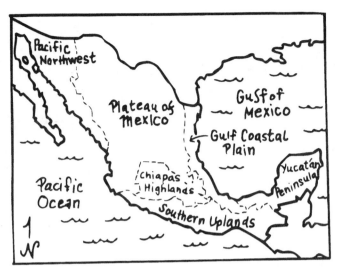

Where in the world can you see deserts, forests, jungles, grasslands, mountains, and volcanoes all in one country? In Mexico, of course!

Mexico is divided into six major regions: the Pacific Northwest, the Plateau of Mexico, the Gulf Coastal Plain, the Southern Uplands, the Chiapas Highlands, and the Yucatán Peninsula. Each region differs in climate, altitude, landforms, and plant and animal life.

The Pacific Northwest is located along the United States border by California and Arizona; it includes Baja California. The southern part of the region is tropical, whereas the northern section is part of the Sonora Desert. Coyotes, lizards, and rattlesnakes live among cacti and thorny shrubs in the desert. Mexico's largest deposits of copper are found in the Pacific Northwest.

The largest region in Mexico is the Plateau of Mexico. It contains most of the population and cities. It is called a plateau because the center of the region is flat while on either side are two mountain ranges: the Sierra Madre Occidental to the west and the Sierra Madre Oriental to the east. Deer and mountain lions live in these mountains. The northern area holds rich mineral deposits of silver, lead, zinc, and iron. The central and southern areas include rivers and fertile farmland. The Plateau also features forests where ebony, mahogany, rosewood, and walnut trees are harvested for furniture.

The Gulf Coastal Plain is covered by tropical rainforests and farmland in the south. Coal, natural gas, and oil are found here. Parts of the Gulf Coast are covered with swamps and lagoons.

The Southern Uplands lie along the Sierra Madre del Sur mountain range. Iron ore and mercury are found in this region. The resort town of Acapulco is on the southwestern coast.

The Chiapas Highlands is a small region of southern Mexico that borders Guatemala. It consists of block-like mountains and flat farmlands.

The Yucatán Peninsula is a low plateau of limestone that is marked with large pits or wells. The northwestern section is dry scrubland. Tropical rainforests, complete with alligators, jaguars, opossums, and monkeys, cover the southern region.

Geography

RESEARCH QUESTIONS

1. Define the following vocabulary words: *altitude, tropical, cacti, deposits* (noun), *plateau, mineral, fertile, mahogany,* and *jaguar.*

2. Find out where the lowest point in Mexico is. (*Hint:* It is somewhere in the Pacific Northwest.)

3. Find out about the ruins of *Monte Albán* in the Southern Uplands. Report your findings to the class using at least two visual aids.

4. *Sapodilla trees* grow in Mexico. Find out where they are grown and what purpose they serve.

5. Research *volcanoes* of Mexico. Where are they located? Are any of them active now? Report your findings to the class.

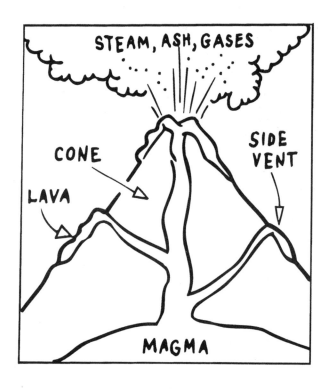

PROJECTS

1. Using salt and flour or clay, make a three-dimensional map of Mexico indicating mountains, deserts, rainforests, and plateaus.

2. Create a series of maps on Mexico. The first map could be on the six regions of Mexico, including major cities in each region; the second indicating plant life and minerals; and the third, showing animal life throughout Mexico.

3. Read more about your favorite region in Mexico. Then write an article on it for the next edition of *Kids-in-the-Know Encyclopedia.*

4. How could the same country have deserts, mountains, rainforests, and jungles? Give reasons to support your answer.

Mexico

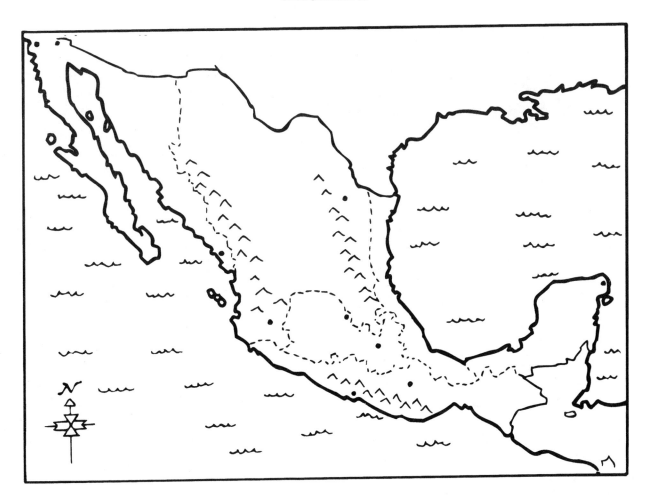

1. Using an encyclopedia, identify the following on your map:
   - Pacific Northwest
   - Plateau of Mexico
   - Gulf Coastal Plain
   - Southern Uplands
   - Chiapas Highlands
   - Yucatán Peninsula
   - Sierra Madre Occidental
   - Sierra Madre del Sur
   - Gulf of California
   - Gulf of Mexico
   - Pacific Ocean
   - Tropic of Cancer
   - Rio Grande River
   - Mexico City
   - Sierra Madre Oriental
   - Guadalajara
   - Mazatlán
   - Cancún
   - Oaxaca
   - Querétaro
   - Tijuana
   - Mexicali
   - Acapulco
   - Monterrey

2. If the Tropic of Cancer passes through Mexico, then you know that you are near 0° latitude, or the_____

3. If you lived in Mexico, in which region would you like to live?
   _____

   Give at least three reasons for your answer.
   _____
   _____
   _____
   _____
   _____

The Maya

The Mayan civilization covered part of what is now Central America, including Mexico's Yucatán Peninsula, Guatemala, Belize, El Salvador, and a section of Honduras. Much of the land was forest and mountains.

Historians believe that Mayan history began around A.D. 320. Important Mayan cities in Mexico were Tikal, Palenque, Uxmal, and Chichén Itzá.

Mayan society was divided into four groups: the ruling class, priests, craftsmen, and common farmers. There was no king because local leaders in each area formed the ruling class.

The Maya wore distinctive clothing. Men wore plain white cotton clothing and brass or copper cuffs on their ankles and wrists. The clothing of wealthy men was embroidered with bright colors. Men also wore noseplugs, earplugs, and cuffs made of gold or silver as a sign of wealth. Men burned their hair to create a bald spot on the top of their heads; they grew the rest of their hair long.

Mayan women also wore plain white cotton clothing and decorated themselves with metal jewelry. They parted their hair in the middle and wore it braided. Women often tattooed the upper half of their bodies as a sign of beauty. Both men and women filed their teeth and inserted metal plates into their lips for special occasions.

The Maya believed in hundreds of gods, most of them from nature. Sacrifices to keep the gods happy included birds and small animals as well as humans.

Corn was the main food for the Maya, as well as other vegetables, fish, and fowl. Each family also kept bees for honey in order to sweeten food.

A typical Mayan house was a one-room hut with no windows and one door. The upper class lived in the cities in palaces made of stucco.

A favorite sport of the Maya was a game similar to today's soccer. Two teams tried to drive a leather ball through a ring high on the side of the court. Players could not touch the ball with their hands, but could use their feet, elbows, wrists, and hips.

The Maya were fascinated with time. They developed a 365-day calendar according to star charts read by astronomers.

No one knows why the Mayan civilization declined in 900. Experts suggest disease, overpopulation, crop failures, or invaders as possible reasons.

The Maya

RESEARCH QUESTIONS

1. Define the following vocabulary words: *distinctive, embroider, insert, fowl, stucco, fascinated,* and *astronomer*.

2. On a map of Mexico and Central America, identify the area of the Mayan civilization. Also identify the cities of Tikal, Palenque, Uxmal, and Chichén Itzá.

3. The Maya had an interesting way to record important dates and events. Research *stele* monuments, and report your findings to the class using at least three visual aids.

4. Create a timeline for the Mayan civilization. Also indicate the times for the great city of Teotihuacán near Tenochtitlán (now Mexico City) and the Aztec Empire.

5. Research Mayan marriage and burial procedures. Present your findings in a three-page report with at least two visual aids.

6. Find out more about Mayan scientific and mathematical discoveries. Compare the Mayan calendar to the Aztec calendar for similarities and differences.

PROJECTS

1. Read more about Mayan clothing and design. Make clothing for dolls as either wealthy or poor Mayans.

2. Why do you think the Mayans preferred cotton clothing?

3. The Maya were the first known civilization to develop the concept of *zero* in mathematics. Why was that important?

4. The mathematics system of the Maya was based on twenty. On what is ours based?

5. Plan and write a menu for an important Mayan occasion.

Aztecs

According to Aztec legend, a sun god called the Hummingbird Wizard directed ancient Aztec people to leave their homeland of Aztlán in A.D. 1168. The Hummingbird Wizard told his people to travel south into the Valley of Mexico and make their homes where they saw an eagle devouring a snake while sitting on a cactus, or *tenochltli*. They found the eagle on an island in Lake Texcoco, and called their city Tenochtitlán (tay-nak-teet-LAN) or "place of the cactus." The Aztec filled in the lake with mud and built their city in the middle of Lake Texcoco. In time, the Aztec Empire included much of central and southern Mexico.

Religion played a major role in the life of every Aztec. It involved group ceremonies performed to please their gods. Many of their ceremonies required human sacrifices.

The Aztecs had four major social classes: the king and high priests, the merchants and craftsmen, the poor, and slaves. The majority of people were poor farmers who lived in family units called clans. Each clan had its own leaders, priests, and schools. Male clan members either served in the army or worked on farms or buildings. Women took care of the children and households.

Aztec clothing was a sign of social class. Poor women wore ankle-length skirts and over-sized blouses. Peasant men wore loin cloths and a cloak called a *tilmantli* tied over their right shoulders. Upper-class merchants wore their *tilmantli* tied under their chins, while wealthy women wore flowing dresses with fine jewelry and headdresses. Priests wore black hooded cloaks.

The Aztecs spoke the *Nahuatl* language. They used a form of picture writing called glyphs. They created a 360-day calendar, which is on view today in the Museum of Anthropology in Mexico City. This calendar also foretold solar eclipses and great earthquakes.

The Aztec Empire came to an abrupt end in 1521 when Hernán Cortés of Spain fooled Aztec ruler Montezuma II into thinking that Cortés was a god. The Spanish conquered and nearly wiped out the Aztecs, due to superior weapons and deadly diseases brought by the Europeans to the New World.

Aztecs

RESEARCH QUESTIONS

1. Define the following vocabulary words: *devour, sacrifice, clan, headdress, glyph, anthropology, abrupt,* and *superior.*

2. Research the marriage customs of the Aztecs. What is the original meaning of "tying the knot" when referring to marriage?

3. Draw a map of the city of Tenochtitlán in Lake Texcoco. Be sure to include the bridge-like *causeways* that connected the capital city to its sister cities of Tepeyac, Tlacopán, Chapultepec, Coyoacán, Churubusco, Acachinaneo, Culhuacan, and Ixtapalapa.

4. Find out more about Aztec religious practices. Present your findings to the class using at least two visual aids.

PROJECTS

1. Find a picture of the Mexican flag. Of what significance is the emblem on the flag? In your own words, write the story behind the emblem and state why you think it was chosen as a national symbol for the Mexican flag.

2. In books find pictures of typical Aztec homes. Then draw a poster showing a wealthy Aztec palace as well as a poor farmer's hut.

3. Find a copy of the fresco painting *Great Tenochtitlán* by Diego Rivera, located in the National Palace in Mexico City. If you had lived back then, who would you have been in the painting? Write a story about your life as an Aztec in Tenochtitlán.

4. What major city of today is built on the ruins of Tenochtitlán?

The End of the Aztec Empire

Put the sentences in logical order to find out how the Aztec Empire was conquered.

_____ Believing that Cortés was a god, Montezuma welcomed Cortés to Tenochtitlán.

_____ Aztec legend stated that a white-skinned, bearded god named Quetzalcóatl sailed away from Mexico, but promised to return someday from the east.

_____ The Spaniards took over Tenochtitlán, and the Aztec Empire ended.

_____ Messengers alerted Montezuma that white-skinned, bearded men had arrived from the east.

_____ Cortés and his men put Montezuma in chains to show the Aztecs that their leader had been captured and that they should surrender willingly to the Spaniards.

_____ Spanish conquistador Hernán Cortés arrived in Mexico in 1519.

_____ The Aztecs lost respect for the chained Montezuma. They rioted, and Montezuma died, either killed by the Spaniards or by his own people.

_____ After burning his ships, Cortés led his 503 soldiers to Tenochtitlán.

_____ Montezuma read omens saying that Quetzalcóatl was returning to Mexico in 1519 to reclaim his kingdom.

Extra Credit
Why did Cortés burn his ships before marching on Tenochtitlán?

Mexican Pyramids

Everyone knows that there are pyramids in Egypt. Did you know that there are pyramids in Mexico, too?

The Mayan Empire existed mainly on the Yucatán Peninsula. Today tourists visit Mayan pyramids at Palenque in Chiapas, and Uxmal and Chichén Itzá in the Yucatán.

Chichén Itzá was a major political and religious center for the Mayans. Chichén Itzá means "the mouth of the wells of the Chichén people." Archeologists believe that Chichén Itzá was used from A.D. 600 to 1400, when it was abandoned and a new capital was built at Mayapán.

At Chichén Itzá, the Temple Pyramid of Kukulcán was built to honor Quetzalcóatl, who was known as the Feathered Serpent. The 365 steps to the top of the pyramid suggest that the building was also used to mark time. On the days of the equinox, the sun casts a shadow that looks like a serpent on the north steps.

Another impressive structure at Chichén Itzá is the Temple of the Warriors, complete with columns carved in the likenesses of warriors and serpents. Warriors played a game similar to soccer in the temple, however, the losing team was thrown into the Well of Sacrifice.

During the height of the Mayan civilization in the Yucatán, there was a great city named Teotihuacán (tay-oh-tee-wah-KAN) located 25 miles (40 kilometers) northeast of present day Mexico City. Teotihuacán means "the place where gods are created," and it was the first city of the pre-Columbian civilizations in Central America. It was an important religious and commercial center from 100 B.C. to A.D. 650, when it was looted and burned.

The main street of Teotihuacán, running north and south, was called the Street of the Dead, and it was lined with temples and palaces. Intersecting the Street of the Dead on an east-west street is a temple-palace complex called the Citadel and a huge marketplace called the Great Compound. To the east you can climb the magnificent Pyramid of the Sun, and at the north end of the Street is the smaller Pyramid of the Moon. As well as a religious center, Teotihuacán was also a gathering place for artists such as stone workers, potters, sculptors, and painters who lived in artist colonies according to their craft.

When the Aztecs took over the Valley of México in the 1300s, they considered Teotihuacán a sacred place and worshiped some of the same gods. The only Aztec pyramid not destroyed by the Spanish can be seen today at Santa Cecilia near Mexico City.

Mexican Pyramids

RESEARCH QUESTIONS

1. Define the following vocabulary words: *peninsula, political, religious, abandon, equinox, impressive, pre-Columbian,* and *magnificent.*

2. Research the ruins at either Chichén Itzá or Teotihuacán.

3. On a map of Mexico, identify the locations of the pyramids mentioned in the reading.

4. Make a timeline of the civilizations that built pyramids in Mexico.

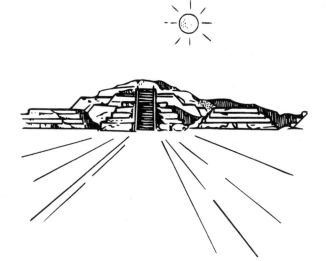

PROJECTS

1. Use resource books to draw either the Temple Pyramid of Kukulcán at Chichén Itzá or the Pyramid of the Sun at Teotihuacán.

2. Make a model of the Temple of the Warriors at Chichén Itzá. Remember to include the Well of Sacrifice.

3. The pyramids in Egypt are very much like the pyramids found in central and eastern Mexico. How could similar pyramids be "invented" on two different continents?

4. The *acoustics* on the plaza in front of the Pyramid of the Sun at Teotihuacán are nearly perfect. Why would it have been important for the architects of the pyramids to create a plaza in which sound could travel well?

5. If you had lived in Teotihuacán, would you have been an artist or a priest? Give at least three reasons for your answer.

Mexican Pyramids Wordfind

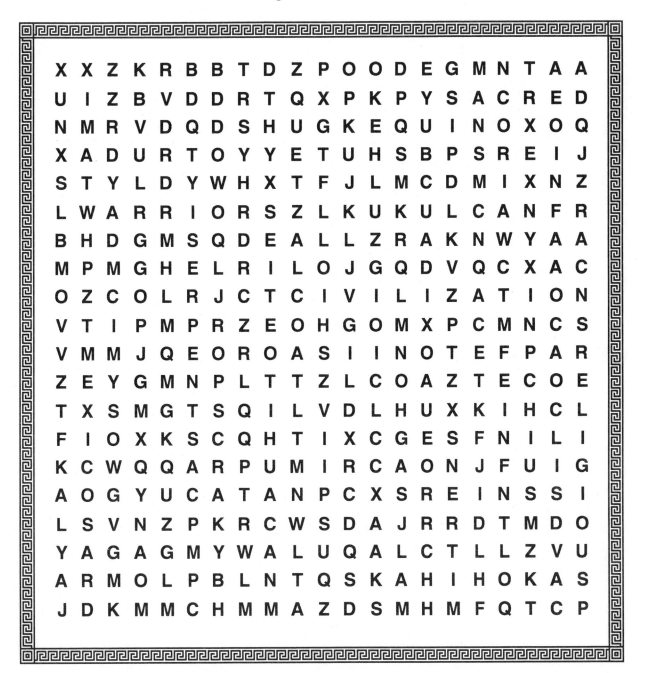

```
X X Z K R B B T D Z P O O D E G M N T A A
U I Z B V D D R T Q X P K P Y S A C R E D
N M R V D Q D S H U G K E Q U I N O X O Q
X A D U R T O Y Y E T U H S B P S R E I J
S T Y L D Y W H X T F J L M C D M I X N Z
L W A R R I O R S Z L K U K U L C A N F R
B H D G M S Q D E A L L Z R A K N W Y A A
M P M G H E L R I L O J G Q D V Q C X A C
O Z C O L R J C T C I V I L I Z A T I O N
V T I P M P R Z E O H G O M X P C M N C S
V M M J Q E O R O A S I I N O T E F P A R
Z E Y G M N P L T T Z L C O A Z T E C O E
T X S M G T S Q I L V D L H U X K I H C L
F I O X K S C Q H T I X C G E S F N I L I
K C W Q Q A R P U M I R C A O N J F U I G
A O G Y U C A T A N P C X S R E I N S S I
L S V N Z P K R C W S D A J R R D T M D O
Y A G A G M Y W A L U Q A L C T L L Z V U
A R M O L P B L N T Q S K A H I H O K A S
J D K M M C H M M A Z D S M H M F Q T C P
```

Can you find these words?

PRE-COLUMBIAN	CIVILIZATION	QUETZALCOATL
TEOTIHUACAN	COMMERCIAL	CHICHEN ITZA
POLITICAL	RELIGIOUS	SACRIFICE
SERPENTS	WARRIORS	KUKULCAN
EQUINOX	PYRAMID	YUCATAN
SACRED	MEXICO	TEMPLE
AZTEC	MAYA	

Mexico City

Mexico City is the second largest city in the world with a population of twenty million people. The city's name in Spanish is *Ciudad de México*. It was founded by Spaniards in 1521 on the site of the Aztec city Tenochtitlán. Mexico City's elevation is 7349 feet (240 meters) above sea level, and it is located in the Valley of México, which was originally the bottom of Lake Texcoco. The Valley of México is surrounded by mountains and covers 571 square miles (1479 square kilometers). The average temperature in summer is 70°F (21°C) and 50°F (10°C) in the winter.

The heart of Mexico City is Constitution Plaza or the Zócalo. It was formerly the center of Tenochtitlán. If you stand in the large public square of the Zócalo, you can see City Hall, the Metropolitan Cathedral (the nation's largest church, it took 250 years to build), and the National Palace, where you can view a series of murals on Mexican history painted by Diego Rivera.

The fabulous Palacio de Bellas Artes (Palace of Fine Arts) is also located in downtown Mexico City, west of the Zócalo on the east side of the Almeda downtown park. The Palacio de Bellas Artes is a performance and exhibition center. It is also the home of the world-famous Ballet Folklorico de Mexico, a dance troupe that specializes in performing ancient Mayan and Aztec dances as well as native folk dances from every region of Mexico.

The Alameda downtown park is located near the Reforma, the main street through Mexico City. If you travel southwest on the Reforma, you will arrive at Chapultepec Park. One of the biggest city parks in the world, Chapultepec includes a castle, five museums, lakes and picnic areas, a zoo, an amusement park, and the home of the president of Mexico. It was originally the location of Montezuma's summer home.

Mexico City also provides a variety of sporting events, such as baseball, boxing, bullfighting, football, horse racing, jai alai, soccer, swimming, and tennis. The most popular sport is soccer, which can be watched by 100,000 fans in Azteca Stadium.

Mexico City is beautiful, but it has some problems common to big cities. Because of its large population, residents deal with crime, pollution, inadequate transportation, and poverty.

Many people are working constantly to improve living conditions and make Mexico City a safe place for all its residents.

Mexico City

RESEARCH QUESTIONS

1. Define the following vocabulary words: *fabulous, specialize, formerly, resident, pollution, inadequate,* and *poverty.*

2. Using resource books, draw a map of downtown Mexico City. Include: the Reforma, the Alameda, Constitution Plaza, Chapultepec Park, and the locations of the Palacio de Bellas Artes, City Hall, the Metropolitan Cathedral, the National Palace, the Plaza of Three Cultures, Azteca Stadium in University City, and the Basilica of Our Lady of Guadeloupe.

3. There are six white columns and a memorial in Chapultepec Park called the "Monument to Niños Héroes." Find out who were the *niños héroes* and why there is a monument to them in Chapultepec Park. Report your findings to the group as if you had watched the event yourself.

4. In downtown Mexico City, there is an area called the *Plaza of Three Cultures.* Find out which three cultures are involved, and write a paragraph describing the plaza.

PROJECTS

1. Imagine that you are a weather broadcaster for a Mexico City television station. Write a weather forecast for July 25 and another for December 25.

2. Using resource books, find pictures of the beautiful Tiffany curtain on the stage of the Palacio de Bellas Artes. Determine the identity of *Tiffany* and why the curtain is famous. Then draw a full-color picture of the curtain and write a paragraph on the backside describing the history of the curtain.

3. You have your choice of going to the boat races in Chapultepec Park or taking a ride on the boats through the streets of Xochimilco (so-shee-MEEL-ko) while *mariachi* bands float past. Which will you choose? Give at least three reasons for your answer.

4. There is a famous mural on the side of Azteca Stadium painted by Diego Rivera. Find a picture of it in a resource book. If you were asked to paint a mural on the side of Azteca Stadium, what would you paint? Draw the plan for your mural.

Bulls or Ballet?

You have a problem. You and your business partner agreed to design a poster for the new show of the Ballet Folklorico and also for the next bullfight. The trouble is that both entertainments will be held next Sunday, which means that both posters have to be designed TODAY! You agree to design the poster for one event and your partner will design the other.

Draw the design for one of the events. The Ballet Folklorico will perform at 9:30 a.m. and 2:30 p.m. in the Palacio de Bellas Artes on Sunday. The bullfight will begin at 4:00 p.m. on Sunday and will be held at the Plaza de Toros Monumental México. As well as drawing the design, you also have to color it. Hurry up—the printing presses are running!

Art and Music

The arts have been alive in Mexico since before Columbus arrived at San Salvador. Examples of pre-Columbian sculpture, pottery, mural paintings, and architecture can be seen today at restored sites such as Teotihuacán and Chichén Itzá, as well as at the Museum of Anthropology located in Chapultepec Park in Mexico City.

After the Spaniards arrived, Mexican culture survived, but it was influenced by European styles. After the Mexican Revolution, artists felt free to express themselves as Mexicans, and their art reflected a sense of national pride. The three major muralists of the times were Diego Rivera, José Clemente Orozco, and David Alfaro Siqueiros.

Contemporary Mexican artists create paintings and murals that are more personal than political or historical. World-renowned Mexican folk art includes silver jewelry, weavings, straw baskets, blue tiles, and works of art in glass, wood, and metals.

Music has also been an important part of Mexican life. Native Mexicans believed that music kept the world in motion and in balance with nature. Music was used in religious ceremonies to educate the people in the ways of the tribe. Different instruments, such as whistles, flutes, drums, shells, rattles, trumpets, and notched deer bones were used to make music.

A style of music very popular in Mexico today is called *nortena*. Sometimes it is known as *ranchero* music because it is sung by ranch hands. It sounds similar to country western music.

The most well-known form of traditional Mexican music is the *mariachi* band. The musicians wear wide *sombreros*, dark suits, frilly shirts, and cowboy boots. These *mariachi* performers play romantic music with violins, guitars, and trumpets as they stroll by party guests or fiesta-goers.

Art and Music

RESEARCH QUESTIONS

1. Define the following vocabulary words: *restore, express, reflect, contemporary, political, historical, renowned, notched, nortena, ranchero, mariachi, sombrero,* and *stroll*.

2. Find out more about the *Museum of Anthropology* in Mexico City. When was it built? How many different native tribes does it feature? Which god is depicted in the huge stone statue standing next to the entrance of the museum? Share your findings with the class as if you were their tour guide on a trip to Mexico City.

3. Research the lives of one of the artists mentioned in the reading: *Diego Rivera, José Orozco,* or *David Siqueiro.* Write a two-page report on him and include a copy of at least one of his murals.

PROJECTS

1. In resource books, look at pictures of the *Palacio de Bellas Artes* (Palace of Fine Arts) in Mexico City. Why do you think that the architecture on the outside of the building is 1890s' Italian style, while the inside is decorated in 1930s' art deco style, and a 1910 art nouveau glass curtain decorates the stage?

2. *Marionette* puppets originated in Spain, but became very popular in Mexico. These puppets can easily be bought in Mexico today. Make your own marionette puppet, complete with strings, and give a puppet show with your friends.

3. The most famous of all Mexican dances is the *Jarabe tapatío*, or the Mexican Hat Dance. Find a recording of the music, a large *sombrero*, a partner, and teach the dance to the class.

4. Listen to a recording of *nortena* music, then to a country western song. Make a list of the similarities and differences between the two styles of music.

Diego Rivera and Frida Kahlo

"I am not sick. I am broken. But I am happy to be alive as long as I can paint."
Frida Kahlo

Born on December 8, 1886, Diego Rivera was to become one of Mexico's finest painters and muralists. He studied art at the Academy of San Carlos in Mexico City when he was ten years old, and won a scholarship in 1907 to study art in Europe when he was twenty-one. While living in Europe, Rivera became friends with many important modern artists, including Georges Braque and Pablo Picasso.

Rivera decided to return to Mexico in 1921. He wanted to inspire national pride through his art, not by painting for museums and galleries, but by creating murals about the history of Mexicans on the walls of national buildings for all people to see. Rivera expressed his Marxist political beliefs in many of his works.

Rivera was very famous for his style of fresco painting on large walls. With an entire wall as his "canvas," Rivera could tell the stories of the struggles of the Mexican people in mural form. Since many Mexicans could not read or write, Rivera was able to educate people about the past, present, and what he believed to be the future of the Mexican people.

When he was forty-three, Rivera married nineteen-year-old Frida Kahlo, who became a celebrated international painter. Influenced by Rivera, Frida Kahlo based her style on Mexican folk art. Unlike her husband's work, Kahlo's paintings were small and self-reflective. Frida Kahlo was a flamboyant, intense artist who suffered many illnesses and operations. Her paintings depicted her world of beauty and physical pain.

When Frida Kahlo died at the age of forty-seven, Diego Rivera appeared to grow old instantly. He donated his wife's house to the state; it is now called the Frida Kahlo Museum.

Diego Rivera died in Mexico City on November 25, 1957, at the age of seventy-one. Some of his murals are on display at the National Palace and the Palacio de Bellas Artes in Mexico City.

Diego Rivera and Frida Kahlo

RESEARCH QUESTIONS

1. Define the following vocabulary words: *muralist, scholarship, inspire, Marxist, fresco, flamboyant, intense,* and *depict*.

2. Research the life of either *Diego Rivera* or *Frida Kahlo*. Find someone in the class who researched the other one, and give a five-minute presentation to the class on their lives and works.

3. Find out more about Rivera's friends *Georges Braque* and *Pablo Picasso*. Choose one of Braque's or Picasso's artworks, make a copy of it using pencils, paints, or chalk, and attach to the back side of it a paragraph about the original artist.

4. Make a timeline of significant events in the lives of *Diego Rivera* and *Frida Kahlo*.

5. *Fresco* painting did not begin with Diego Rivera. Research the history of fresco painting in Europe and America. Present your findings to the class.

PROJECTS

1. Look at a copy of *Self-Portrait with Monkey 1940* by Frida Kahlo. What is she thinking? Why did Kahlo choose to paint a monkey in her own portrait? What might the ribbons symbolize in her painting?

2. Frida Kahlo was also an art teacher in Mexico City. She encouraged her students to paint what they felt as well as what they saw. Draw a *thumbnail sketch*, or pencil drawing, to show what you saw and felt on your last birthday.

3. Find a photograph of Diego Rivera. Describe the features of his face to a friend and see if your friend can accurately draw a portrait of Diego Rivera.

4. Diego Rivera painted a mural for Rockefeller Center in New York City, but it was destroyed—on purpose! Find out why, and present your findings to the class as if you were a television news reporter.

Murals, Mexican-Style

The murals of Diego Rivera and other leading artists of his time told the history of the people of Mexico. You can be an artist of history yourself! You will need:

- A planned drawing, completely colored
- A large surface, such as a long sheet of white butcher paper, a sidewalk, or a wall of a building (indoor or outdoor)
- Paint or colored chalk

1. Look in resource books to see what kinds of murals Diego Rivera painted.

2. As a group, decide what you want to express in your mural. On a sheet of paper not smaller than 18" x 24", draw an important event that happened in your school, town, state, or country.

3. Gather together everyone's drawings and decide on the final plan for your mural. Choose someone from the group to draw the final plan and choose someone else to color it.

4. Decide which group-members will draw which sections of the class mural onto the large surface and who will color it.

5. Choose someone to prepare the paints and brushes or gather the colored chalks.

6. Choose a cleanup crew.

7. Choose one person or a small group to prepare a short speech on the significance of your class mural. This speech will be given at the mural dedication ceremony.

8. Using the final plan, draw the mural in sections. Make sure that each artist is aware of what the other artists are drawing so that the completed mural will be in proportion.

9. Complete the mural by coloring it.

10. Invite the entire school to the mural dedication ceremony.

Fiestas

Who does not like a good party? Mexicans are no exception. Mexico celebrates more fiestas than any other Latin American country.

Religious fiestas are important celebration days. One such fiesta is Guadaloupe Day on December 12. It celebrates the day in 1531 when the Virgin Mary is said to have appeared before a man named Juan Diego. The Virgin Mary asked that a church be built on the top of the hill outside of Mexico City on which they were standing. On December 12, people come from all over the country to the shrine on the hill hoping for a miracle from the Virgin.

For nine days before Christmas, Mexicans perform *posadas*, or reenactments of the journey of Mary and Joseph to Bethlehem. After a *posada*, the children are allowed to break open a *piñata*, a papier-mâché container filled with candy and toys.

Another important religious festival is *El día de los muertos* (Day of the Dead), recalling family members and loved ones who have died. On October 31, candies shaped into skulls, toy skeletons, and coffins are left out with hot chocolate for the *muertitos chicos* (souls of dead children), to sweeten their visit to earth. The following evening the adult souls are believed to visit, so the adults' favorite foods are prepared for them. November 2nd is the official Day of the Dead, and everyone celebrates by eating the foods and carrying golden marigolds to the town cemetery for an all-night candlelight vigil by the graves of family members.

Patriotic fiestas are also celebrated in Mexico. *Cinco de Mayo*, on the fifth of May, recalls the Battle of Puebla in 1862, when Mexican peasants defeated the French army. It is celebrated with a speech from the President and a military parade in Mexico City.

Another important patriotic day is Independence Day on September 16, the date in 1810 when Father Hidalgo proclaimed Mexico's independence from Spain. Independence Day begins on September 15 with a reenactment of Father Hidalgo's battlecry *El grito de dolores* (Cry of Sorrows). The festivities continue through September 16 with speeches, food, music, dancing, and ending with fireworks in the evening.

Fiestas

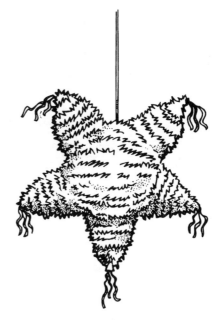

RESEARCH QUESTIONS

1. Define the following vocabulary words: *fiesta, religious, reenactment, posada, piñata, coffin, muertitos chicos, marigold, vigil, patriotic,* and *battlecry.*

2. Research the story about the Virgin of Guadaloupe. Present your findings to the class using at least two visual aids.

3. Research the *Battle of Puebla*. Make a model showing who fought whom and tell the class about the battle and its outcome.

4. Find out more about *Father Miguel Hidalgo* and *El grito de dolores*. Present your findings in a written report between two and four pages, including at least one picture.

5. There is an unusual custom practiced on Corpus Christi Day. Find out about the "Flying Pole Dance" and report your findings back to the group.

PROJECTS

1. Make a calendar of important Mexican fiestas and festivals. Include a small picture and write a one-sentence description for each event.

2. Find examples of skeleton diorama created for *El día de los muertos* (moo-ER-tos). Then make your own diorama of skeletons.

3. Make a *piñata* using a balloon, newspaper, papier-mâché paste, and paints. Do not forget to put candy into it when you are done!

4. October 12 in Mexico is called *El día de la Raza* (Day of the Race). What is significant about that day in the United States? in Mexico?

5. Why do Mexicans always use marigolds during the ceremonies for *El día de los muertos*? Find out, then give a flower to someone who is important to you.

6. List the ingredients for the perfect *piñata*.

Fiestas Crossword Puzzle

ACROSS

1. The souls of the dead children who visit earth again on the Day of the Dead
5. Battle on May 5, 1862, when Mexican peasants rose up against French soldiers
6. A holy place; an example in Mexico is on the hill where the Virgin Mary is said to have appeared
7. Country south of the United States and north of Guatemala
8. A papier-mâché container filled with candy and toys
9. A celebration or festival
13. Number of days the *posadas* are performed in Mexico
14. To act out an event again
15. Celebrated every December 12, it recalls the day when the Virgin Mary appeared to a man
16. Reenactment of the journey of Mary and Joseph to Bethlehem
17. Type of flower used to decorate graves at cemeteries on the Day of the Dead

DOWN

2. September 16, the day when Mexico declared independence from Spain
3. He sounded the famous battlecry that inspired Mexican peasants to rebel against the Spanish
4. A festival in Mexico that remembers family members and loved ones who have died
11. Name of the man who saw the Virgin Mary on a hill outside Mexico City
10. The last festivities on Mexico's independence Day (occurs at night)
12. The fifth of May, day when Mexican peasants defeated the French Army

Village Life, City Life

Life in a remote Mexican village today is not much different than it was years ago. There are villages in the mountains of Mexico that still do not have electricity, a reliable water supply, or sanitary facilities. Houses are built out of adobe brick and consist of one windowless room in which the entire family, including grandparents and other relatives, sleeps and eats.

The basic food of villagers is the *tortilla*. Most villages have mills that grind corn into meal for the *tortillas*. Women rise before dawn to shape and toast the *tortillas* that the men will take to work for their noon meal. For each person, twenty *tortillas* filled with a homemade sauce of chilies are normal. The foods eaten for breakfast, lunch, and dinner are often the same. In addition to *tortillas* and chili sauce, there may be rice, beans, squash, homegrown fruit, and tea or coffee to drink. Eggs, poultry, and meat are only for special occasions.

Families are large so that there are more people to work in the fields, haul firewood and water, prepare food, take care of the little ones or the sick, clean the house, and weave rope and cloth for clothing. In traditional village families, the father is the head of the family. The mother is a full-time caretaker and is respected for her dedication to her family. Girls usually marry around age sixteen, boys at age twenty. Boys are expected to be tough and independent. Girls are taught to be obedient wives and good mothers.

Many young people living in villages long for the glamour and opportunities of city life. Some of them choose to leave their villages for the bright lights of Mexico City, Guadalajara, Acapulco, Oaxaca, Querétaro, and other large cities. However, city life offers challenges as well. Many villagers find upon arriving in a large city that work is not easy to find. They often stay temporarily with relatives in overcrowded tenements until they can find a small, one-room apartment of their own. Education is mandatory; however, many boys work to help support their families.

There is a small but important group of people in Mexico who live as comfortably as middle-class Americans. This financially-comfortable group have homes with all the modern conveniences, own their own cars, travel with their families on vacations, and even have live-in servants. These are the people shaping the country today, and they send both their sons and daughters to private schools and abroad to the United States and Europe in order to prepare them for well-paying careers. The expectation is that once the children are educated, they will return to Mexico and work toward improving the quality of life for all.

Village Life, City Life

RESEARCH QUESTIONS

1. Define the following vocabulary words: *remote, electricity, reliable, sanitary, facilities, adobe, haul, dedication, obedient, glamour, opportunities, temporarily, tenement, mandatory, conveniences, abroad,* and *expectation.*

2. Choose one of the cities mentioned in the reading: *Mexico City, Guadalajara, Acapulco, Oaxaca,* or *Querétaro.* Find out more about the city, including location, population, and any unusual facts that you find interesting. Report your information to the class.

3. Find out more about city life and village life. Then make a chart showing the similarities and differences between life in the city and the country.

4. Research the dating rituals of Mexican young people today. Write your findings in a two-page report, ending with your opinions on the topic.

6. Research the customs of a girl's fifteenth birthday. Why do you think the families do so much for a girl when she turns fifteen? Report your findings to the class using at least two visual aids.

PROJECTS

1. Learn how to count in Spanish.

2. Using resource books, draw a picture of a traditional Mexican boy and girl in authentic dress clothes. Then draw another picture of a modern Mexican boy and girl in typical clothes worn today.

3. You are a poor fourteen-year-old Mexican boy. You know that the only way you can get a good job is to go to school so that you can win a scholarship to a university, but your parents need help in supporting your grandparents and nine brothers and sisters. What will you do?

4. You are a sixteen-year-old Mexican girl living in Mexico City. Your father wants you to go to school in the United States so that you can become a doctor and then get married. You are taught to obey your father in all things, but you really want to play basketball on the national women's basketball team, and someday compete in the Olympics. Marriage, children, and being a doctor is not at all what you want out of life. What will you do?

5. Mexicans use the *peso* as the basic form of money. How many *pesos* equal one dollar?

It's Taco Time!

The most popular food in Mexico is a tortilla filled with tasty treats. Here are the recipes for soft tortillas and taco filling:

Tortillas

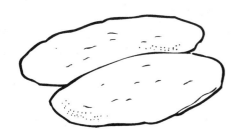

1½ cups cold water
1 cup all-purpose flour
½ cup cornmeal
¼ teaspoon salt
1 egg

Heat 8-inch skillet over medium-low heat just until hot. Grease skillet if necessary.

Beat water, flour, cornmeal, salt, and egg with hand beater until smooth. Pour ¼ cup of the batter into skillet; immediately rotate skillet until batter forms very thin tortilla about six inches in diameter. Cook tortilla until dry around edge, about two minutes. Turn and cook other side until golden, about two minutes longer. Cool tortillas. Makes about one dozen.

Taco Filling

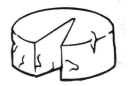

8 tortillas
1 pound hamburger
1 cup water
1 medium onion, chopped (about ½ cup)
2 tablespoons chili powder
1 teaspoon salt
1 clove garlic, crushed
1 cup lettuce, shredded
1 large tomato, chopped (about 1 cup)
1 cup cheddar cheese, shredded
½ cup sour cream

Prepare tortillas. Cook and stir hamburger in 10-inch skillet until light brown; drain. Stir in water, onion, chili powder, salt, and garlic. Heat to boiling; reduce heat. Simmer uncovered, stirring occasionally, until thickened, about ten minutes.

Spoon about ¼ cup hamburger mixture into center of each tortilla. Top with shredded lettuce, chopped tomato, shredded cheese, and sour cream. Fold tortilla and eat. Makes about eight tacos.

Mexico Timeline

8000 B.C.	Nomads cross Bering Strait and travel south through North and Central America
1200–400 B.C.	Olmec Indians live along Gulf Coast
300 B.C.–A.D. 900	Mayan Indians live in Gulf Coast and Yucatán regions
A.D. 250–900	Civilization flourishes at city of Teotihuacán in Valley of México
A.D. 600–1400	City of Chichén Itzá thrives in the Yucatán
900 –1200	Toltec Indians controlled Valley of México
1325–1521	Aztec empire rules Valley of México
1521–1810	Spaniards conquer and rule Mexico
1810–1821	Mexican War for independence from Spain
1824	Mexico becomes a republic
1846–1847	Mexican War with the United States
1864–1867	France invades and rules Mexico
1910–1914	Revolution of 1910
1917	Constitution signed, guaranteeing rights of individuals
1985	Devastating earthquakes hit Mexico City
1993	North American Free Trade Agreement signed with United States and Canada; Mexican workers rebel

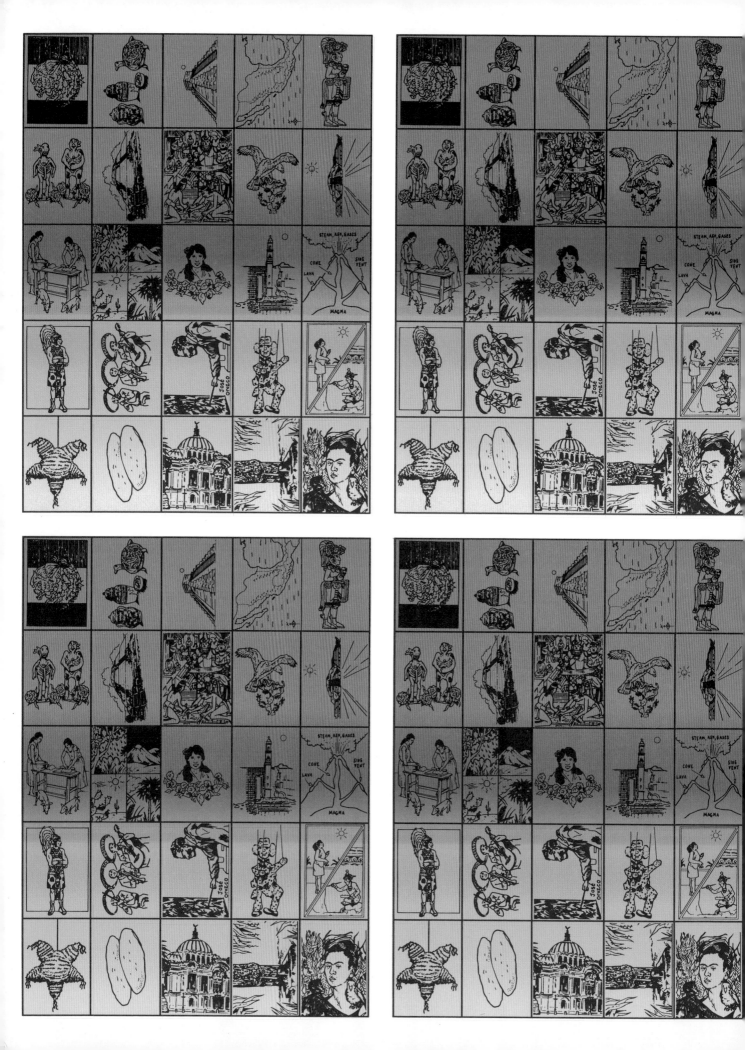